Blastoff! Readers are carefully developed by literacy experts to build reading stamina and move students toward fluency by combining standards-based content with developmentally appropriate text.

LEVELS

Level 1 provides the most support through repetition of high-frequency words, light text, predictable sentence patterns, and strong visual support.

Level 2 offers early readers a bit more challenge through varied sentences, increased text load, and text-supportive special features.

Level 3 advances early-fluent readers toward fluency through increased text load, less reliance on photos, advancing concepts, longer sentences, and more complex special features.

★ **Blastoff! Universe**

Reading Level

Grade K

Grades 1–3

Grade 4

This edition first published in 2025 by Bellwether Media, Inc.

No part of this publication may be reproduced in whole or in part without written permission of the publisher. For information regarding permission, write to Bellwether Media, Inc., Attention: Permissions Department, 6012 Blue Circle Drive, Minnetonka, MN 55343.

Library of Congress Cataloging-in-Publication Data

LC record for Shy available at: https://lccn.loc.gov/2024014727

Text copyright © 2025 by Bellwether Media, Inc. BLASTOFF! READERS and associated logos are trademarks and/or registered trademarks of Bellwether Media, Inc. Bellwether Media is a division of Chrysalis Education Group.

Editor: Rebecca Sabelko   Designer: Andrea Schneider

Printed in the United States of America, North Mankato, MN.

Table of Contents

New People	4
What Is Shyness?	6
Being Shy	14
Glossary	22
To Learn More	23
Index	24

New People

Grace is at
a birthday party.
There are many
new people.
She feels shy.

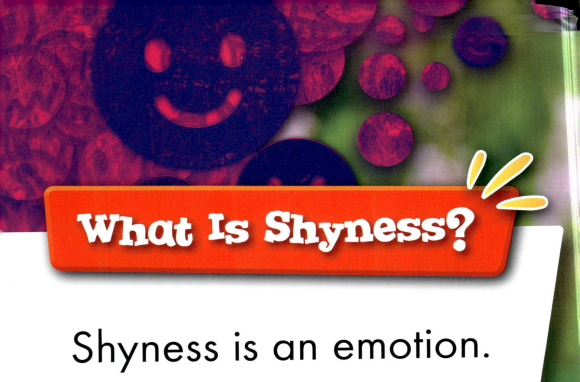

What Is Shyness?

Shyness is an emotion. It can feel scary and **awkward** to be shy.

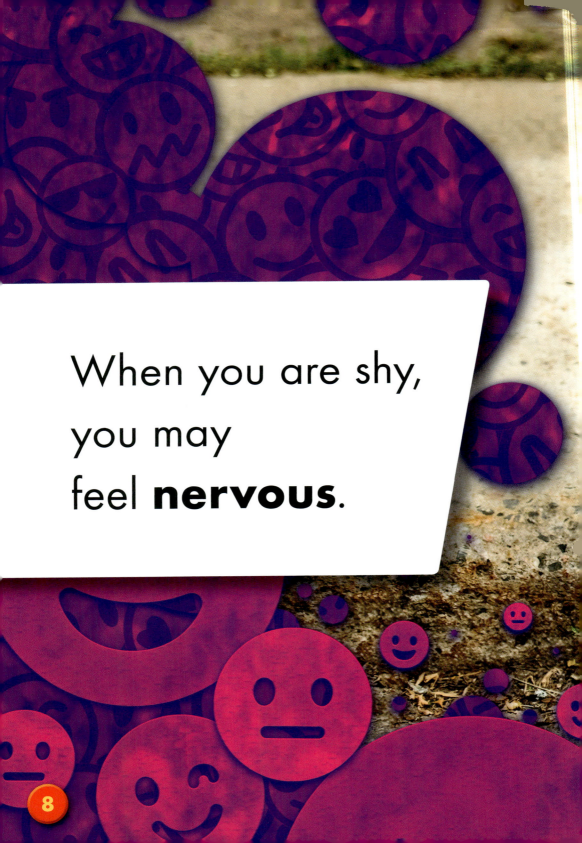

When you are shy, you may feel **nervous**.

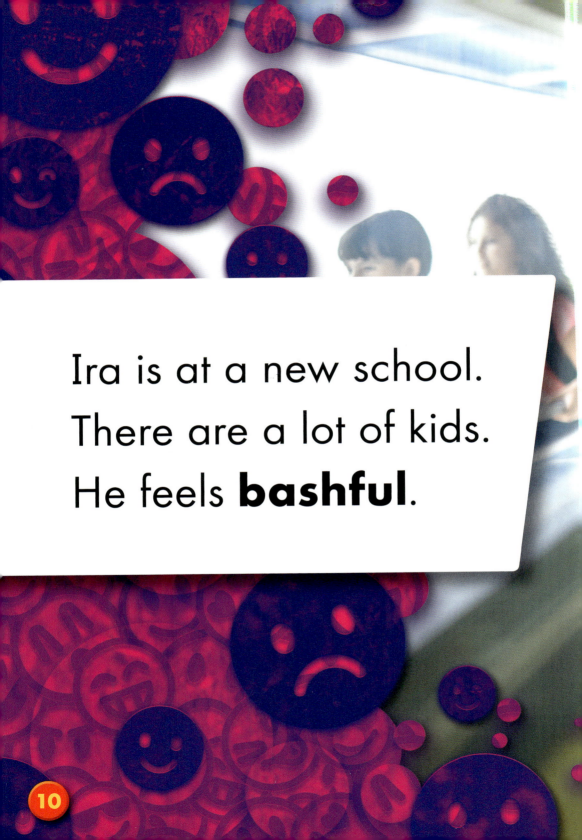

Ira is at a new school. There are a lot of kids. He feels **bashful**.

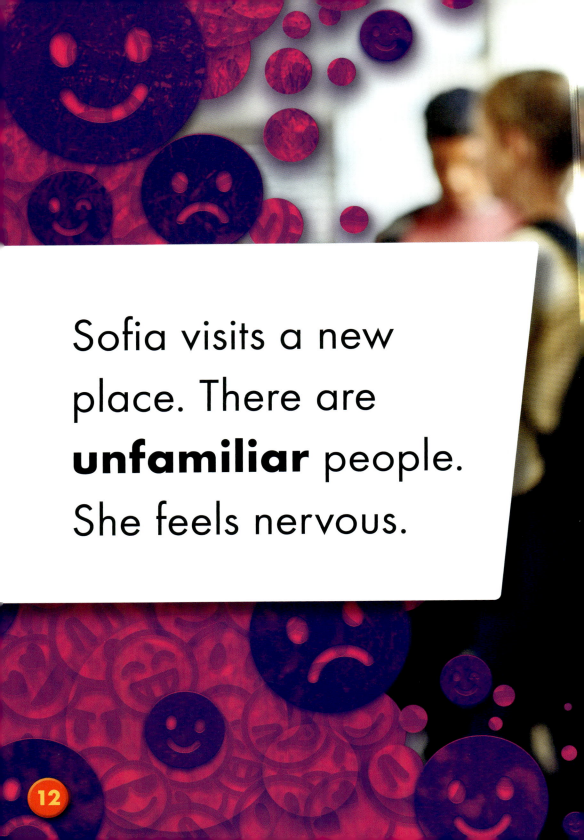

Sofia visits a new place. There are **unfamiliar** people. She feels nervous.

Why Are You Shy?

being at a party

starting at a new school

being near unfamiliar people

Being Shy

Max feels shy.
He is quiet. He looks down at his feet.

Alice feels bashful. She hides behind her mom.

We all feel shy sometimes. It is okay to need **comfort**.

Try talking to an adult you trust. Tell them why you feel shy.

Glossary

awkward

unsure or uncomfortable

nervous

uncomfortable or fearful

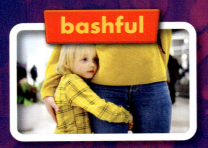

bashful

nervous or uncomfortable around other people

unfamiliar

not well known

comfort

actions that help a person feel better or more comfortable

To Learn More

AT THE LIBRARY

Chang, Kirsten. *Understanding Emotions*. Minneapolis, Minn.: Bellwether Media, 2022.

Finne, Stephanie. *I Feel Shy*. Minneapolis, Minn.: Jump!, 2022.

Lindeen, Mary. *Feeling Shy*. Chicago, Ill.: Norwood House Press, 2022.

ON THE WEB

FACTSURFER

Factsurfer.com gives you a safe, fun way to find more information.

1. Go to www.factsurfer.com.
2. Enter "shy" into the search box and click 🔍.
3. Select your book cover to see a list of related content.

Index

adult, 20
awkward, 6
bashful, 10, 16
comfort, 18, 19
emotion, 6
feels, 4, 6, 8, 10, 12, 14, 16, 18, 20
hides, 16
identify shyness, 17
kids, 10
looks down, 14
nervous, 8, 12
new, 4, 10, 12
party, 4

people, 4, 12
place, 12
question, 21
quiet, 14
scary, 6
school, 10
talking, 20
why are you shy, 13

The images in this book are reproduced through the courtesy of: Patrick Foto, front cover (shy child); Lightfieldstudiosprod, front cover (background); sharplaninac, p. 3; SeventyFour, pp. 4-5, 13 (being near unfamiliar people); Alinute Silzeviciute, pp. 6-7; LSOphoto, pp. 8-9; FG Trade, pp. 10-11; LumiNola, pp. 12-13; BigPixel Photo, p. 13 (being at a party); xavierarnau, p. 13 (starting at a new school); soupstock, pp. 14-15; olenachukhil, pp. 16-17; GOLFX, p. 17 (being quiet); Nicoleta Ionescu, p. 17 (looking down); JGalione, p. 17 (hiding); Lopolo, pp. 18-19; dragana991, pp. 20-21; Stella_E, p. 22 (awkward); SbytovaMN, p. 22 (bashful); bmcent1, p. 22 (comfort); Krakenimages.com, p. 22 (nervous); Thai Liang Lim, p. 22 (unfamiliar); Gelpi, p. 22 (shy child).